Hugh Farrar McDermott

Poems from an Editor's Table

Hugh Farrar McDermott

Poems from an Editor's Table

ISBN/EAN: 9783743305083

Manufactured in Europe, USA, Canada, Australia, Japa

Cover: Foto ©ninafisch / pixelio.de

Manufactured and distributed by brebook publishing software (www.brebook.com)

Hugh Farrar McDermott

Poems from an Editor's Table

INTRODUCTION.

THINKING —hardly believing—that, from their reception by the press and public, three or four poems in this volume might live a few years, it has been my wish to place them before the reader in a more enduring form.

Our civilization is honesty and truth. These I seek in myself, to promote in others.

THE AUTHOR.

ERRATA.

Page 27—line 5, "learned thee" should be "learnedst thou."

Page 28—line 8, "came thee" should be "cam'st thou."

———— line 14, "doth" should be "dost."

———

A new and improved edition, with several additional poems, is now in preparation.

And I'm passing fast away.

DO NOT SING THAT SONG AGAIN.

On the dark and downward streams
I'm a wreck of idle dreams,
And it puts me on the rack
At the weary looking back,
At the ebb and at the flow,
  In the long, long ago.

Do not sing that song again,
There's a tear in its refrain;
It brings sadly back the time
When my manhood felt its prime,
When the comrades, dear and true,
Closer, warmer, fonder grew,
In the hour of friendship's proof,
When the false ones stood aloof,
And their friendship was but show,
  In the long, long ago.

Do not sing that song again,
It distracts my weary brain;
Ah! too well, alas! I know
It is time for me to go,

And to leave to younger eyes
The mild mystery of the skies,
And this mighty world I tread,
And the grander age ahead.

There's a mist upon the river,
   And there's bleakness on the shore,
And in dreams I pass forever,
   While sad music wafts me o'er.

THE CLOSE.

THE dew of the evening came down
    On cottage and village and town:
It came like a prayer on the sun-burdened air,
    And rested on rest as a crown.

    There was peace in the haze on the hill,
    There was peace in the rhyme of the rill;
And the robin's rich note on the air was afloat,
    With a chirp, and a song, and a trill.

    Though she passed long ago from my mind,
    Though she left me in sadness behind,
She came back to me true in the fall of the dew,
    Once again our affections to bind.

    There was peace in the gloom on my breast,
    As I looked to the far-sinking West;
In that dreamland I gazed on bright altars that blazed
    As beacons where the weary found rest.

THE CLOSE.

In the dew of the evening that fell
    On mountain and streamlet and dell,
Proud hopes of the past before me were cast,
    Their tales of disaster to tell.

I was glad that the close of my day
    And my darkness was not far away;
And my eyelids were wet, but not with regret,
    In the twilight of longings' decay.

And the dew of my dreaming it fell
    On the ashes within my heart's cell;
And the eve of life's close drooped her head in repose,
    As she whispered, "All yet shall be well!"

I SHALL WRAP ME IN DREAMS.

 SHALL wrap me in dreams of the sweetest
and fairest,
The brightest of darlings e'er seen on the earth;
I shall wrap me in dreams of the choicest and rarest—
The rarest of beauties since beauty had birth.

I shall toss on my couch until closely I hold her
In the pride of my heart, in the joy of my breast;
Though her jewels and laces far from me infold her,
All the night by my side my own darling shall rest.

The cares of the day I shall leave for the morrow,
And my thoughts in love's bosom shall calmly repose,
While from me depart all the sin and the sorrow,
Till my dreams are as sweet as the balm of the rose.

O, the soft down of love shall descend on my pillow
    From planets of angels revolving on high;
And, soothing and full as the midsummer billow,
    Adored in my arms my sweet charmer shall lie.

To my true love I'll whisper how fondly I love her,
    I'll prove it with kisses, caresses, and sighs;
O, there is not about her, beyond or above her,
    An angel of grace in affection so wise.

O, there's no joy on earth so strongly abiding
    As dreams of my dear in the stillness of night;
O, there's naught to compare to love sweetly gliding
    From dreams into sleep in a glory of light.

Through the night there's a seraph above my bed beaming,
    And she steals on my lips a kiss and a smile;
And I'm bound by the cords that are spun in my dreaming
    To an angel of truth in whom there's no guile.

I SHALL WRAP ME IN DREAMS.

And so let it be, at the fall of Life's curtain,
    When the last ray of light has fled from my mind,
Though the hopes of my dreams proved always uncertain,
    The cords of my dreaming two spirits shall bind.

THE DAY IS PAST.

THE day is past, the night is here,
   When friendship's tie we sever,
And she we love shall disappear.
   Returning to us never.

So runs the world, through weary years:
   Ere yet our joys are spoken,
The laughing eye is dimmed with tears,
   And tender links are broken.

Oh, sweetest mouth that e'er was made
   To kiss a parting lover:
Oh, fairest cheek that e'er was laid
   Upon a downy cover;

My life you twine in love's embrace,
   Of freedom you deprive me,
And as I dwell on every grace,
   To love's despair you drive me.

Your spirit floats along the air,
  In sunny tides I find it:
And when it fades, the world is bare
  To him it leaves behind it.

IN YOUTH.

IN youth we rested on the hill of Hope,
    And viewed before us the prospective pleasure;
We watched the warm East bathing vale and slope
    With rays downladen with their golden treasure.

There came a shade that lent a tinge to sadness,
    Yet made the soul more spiritually bright;
She took my hand, and in a voice of gladness,
    Pointed to where a bird sailed in the light.

With the swift waving wing that skimmed the air,
    Upward and onward my heart kept time and motion,
Until a cloud, with silvery lining fair,
    Concealed the bird, and blighted my devotion.

The noon approached and with it worldly pain;
  We labored in the vale, with burning rays above
      us;
Slow moved the rook across our field of grain,
  And darkness seemed to fall on those who cared
      to love us.

On the Western slope, in twilight now,
  We turn with sadness to the night behind us;
The care of time is fixed on either brow,
  And sighs are born of thoughts that but remind us.

The bird that sailed, at early summer morn,
  Behind the cloud with silvery lining fair,
Was youth's bright hope, which fled from us with
      scorn,
  And left our days to darkness and despair.

The rook that moved across our field of grain,
  Bore on his wings the blight of coming years;
But still to me there's solace in her strain,
  Who raised me first to life among the spheres.

MY SWEETHEART.

MY sweetheart died in springtime's morning,
    When fields were fair with balmy weather;
When May her bosom was adorning
    With daisies sweet and blooming heather.

On every bough a bird was singing:
    The silky sky uncoiled her tresses;
The blithesome lark was gayly winging
    A flight so bright no song expresses.

My joy went out to greet the wooing
    Of gentle winds and laughing roses,
Their fragrant kiss again renewing,
    Till summer's door the winter closes.

No mate had I for love's caressing,
    No mate had I for love's embraces;
The gay-robed May wore heaven's blessing,
    Reflecting back my lost one's graces.

The mead was green, the hills were rising
 In liquid air, which shone around them;
And Nature, in her nice devising,
 In gauze of dreamy pleasure bound them.

Then lightly stept, the green grass turning,
 A fond one, fled from me forever;
Then on the sward I traced, in mourning:
 "The grave can never true love sever."

In hallowed light I saw her kneeling,
 With pallid cheek and drooping lashes..
Against a ray of old love's feeling
 The vision leaned and fell to ashes.

My sweetheart died in springtime's morning,
 In all her fair and guileless beauty;
Loving her kind, no creature scorning,
 Her sweet, brief life was simple duty.

Forever now a sad bird's singing
 Amid the willows of my sorrow;
And on my dreams the chime is ringing,
 "A better life will dawn to-morrow."

OUR COUNTRY.

ETERNAL empire of the world,
    The first that leads in Freedom's van,
Thy Stars and Stripes shall float unfurl'd
    While God inspires the soul of man.

Thy hills shall shake with Freedom's sound,
    Thy valleys quiver with the shock,
And from the heavens it will rebound,
    Again to peal from dale to rock.

The wild Atlantic leaps with pride,
    The calm Pacific rests in glory,
The music of whose flowing tide
    Is sweetly tuned to Freedom's story.

Like steel that binds the honored oak,
    That marks some spot with sacred care,
Our country's love shall ward the stroke
    That would this hallowed Union share.

Oh, cherished land of holy fame!
  No servile foe shall dare to tread,
While breathes one breath in Freedom's name,
  The sacred soil where martyrs bled.

Through all the space of Freedom's span,
  Liberty knows but one degree—
The noble, honored rank of MAN,
  A name debased save by the free.

SONG OF THE STORM KING.

BLOW, ye winds!
Blow and whistle! Whistle and blow!
There are devils above and devils below!
And I'm King of the Furies wherever I go.

From a little white puff of an argent cloud,
In the summer I spread to a streaming shroud;
From a small, dark spot on the horizon's verge,
In winter I rise to a national dirge.
I stand on the wreck of the mariner's deck,
And I toss to the waves, at the north wind's beck,
The hopes of a voyage from far off lands,
The wails and the woes and the wringing hands;
The babe at the breast and the piercing shriek
Of a wild, mad mother, with stony cheek,
The father, whom time has bent with care,
The lovers, whose hopes were all too fair,

I hurl them away on the billows' foam;
I leave them to Fate, and again I roam.
Oh, blow, ye winds!
Blow and whistle! Whistle and blow!
There are demons above and demons below!
And I'm King of the Furies wherever I go.

I pluck the trees from their steadfast roots,
And fling to the gale the boughs and shoots;
I fill the rivers with rushing floods,
And with spectres fierce I crowd the woods:
They are groves cast out on the turbulent air,
And they feed on the wretches of mad despair;
The steeples I throw from castle and fane,
And laugh at their work who raise them again.
Blow, blow, ye winds!
Blow and whistle! Whistle and blow!
There are demons above and demons below!
And I'm King of the Furies wherever I go.

On my feet are pinions that pull the hills,
And the ropes are black with menacing ills,

Which against the peace of the stars rebel,
And carry from heaven the woes of hell.
My beard is made of the terrors wild
Of houseless mother and freezing child,
I rush over towns with a swoop and a roar;
On hovel and castle my vengeance I pour;
I knock over chimneys and houses unroof,
And laugh at the curses I get in reproof.
Blow, blow, ye winds!
Blow and whistle! Whistle and blow!
There are demons above and demons below!
And I'm King of the Furies wherever I go.

The monarch austere, who sits on his throne,
With terror I shake till I make him groan;
All his squadrons of war that ride on the wave
I send with a blast to a bottomless grave.
I ravage the palace that stands in my path,
And his kingdom I sweep with the hurricane's wrath.
With woe in my eye and black fiends in my blood,
I rush upon all with a pitiless flood.

I seize on the graves, and the coffins up-pull,
And toss to the tempest the death-eaten skull.
The head that to none but its maker would bend,
The limbs that no longer can stand and defend,
The lips that had scoffed at the meek of the earth,
The eyes that once rolled in the pride of high birth,
The brow that had wounded sad hearts by its frown,
And by infamous ways had sought for renown :—
All, all are swept down in the torrent and gale,
And naught's left behind save a dead echo's wail.
Then blow, ye winds!
Blow and whistle! Whistle and blow!
There are devils above and devils below!
And I'm King of the Furies wherever I go.

Wild beasts of the forest I drive in my flight;
The tiger and leopard they skulk from my sight;
The viper and vulture seek shade from the blast—
There's naught save the eagle that's game to the last.
When armies are marshalled in battle array,
One spurt from my charger will set them at bay.

SONG OF THE STORM KING.

I am foe to the earth and foe to the sun,
And from mountain to sea in madness I run.
Sad havoc I make on the hill and the plain,
And I throw from the track the steam-rushing train;
The maimed and the mangled I leave to their woe,
While upward and downward and onward I go.
Through palace and cottage and lady's boudoir,
I rattle and battle and dismally roar.
Oh, blow, ye winds!
Blow and whistle! Whistle and blow!
There are goblins above and goblins below!
And I'm King of the Furies wherever I go.

HOPE ON! HOPE EVER!

LIFT your head above your breast!
    Plant your foot, and raise your chest!
Do not show the chicken heart!
If a man, then bear your part!
You're not here to be a slave!
You're not here to beg and crave!
You were born to wear the crown
Of proud manhood's just renown!
Hope on! Hope ever!
Surrender never!

Should reverses, thick and fast,
Strike your sail at every blast,
Raise your banner, Faith and Will,
And with Hope your canvas fill.
Let your course be honest, true,
And that bent to death pursue.

Never fear but, come what may,
You will find the truth to pay.
Press on! Press ever!
Surrender never!

In your path let nothing stand;
Give the weak a helping hand;
He that's honored in this life,
Aids a brother in the strife;
On the breeze it goes unfurl'd,
One good deed will sway the world.
It is noble, fit, and kind,
Human woes to soothe and bind.
Push on! Push ever!
Surrender never!

You're a man of kingly height,
When your course is in the right;
No man let, however great,
To your manhood dare dictate.
Only tyrants rule the slave!
Only God controls the brave!

Never can a despot rule
In a land of Freedom's school!
Strive on! Strive ever!
Surrender never!

From the soul to man's estate
Stretch the links of human fate;
Let the soul with goodness flow,
That the burnished links may glow,
Till the mind is pure and bright
With a love of truth and right;
Till the heart is beating strong,
Crushing every human wrong.
Hope on! Hope ever!
Surrender never!

HOPE'S ROSE.

I'LL make me a bed in a bunch of roses,
    At the rivulet's feet, where the waters play;
And I'll lay me down where the balm reposes,
    From the shadows that followed me all the day.

The dew on the vale is peacefully falling,
    And the sultry zephyrs in coolness rest:
Long memory's roll, in its sad recalling,
    In a revery soothes my feverish breast.

I pluck me a rose from those that I rest on,
    And far out on the stream I fling it away:
The stream of my dreams my life is a jest on,
    Which rises and sinks, like yon rose on the spray.

My hopes, as yon rose, were bright in their morning,
    And high on the wave of ambition were thrown;
But now they return, no glory adorning,
    To tell me the rose of my morning is flown.

MY BLIND CANARY.

SWEET singer to my dreams,
    My blind canary,
I dwell upon the liquid note
That fills thy little breast and throat,
    And comes forth piping, full and airy,
Reaching far and far away,
To some dreamy, twilight day,
   Whose virgin star with softness beams
     On fairy dell and fairy.

  When night kneels down before the West
    In silent prayer,
That, till the morn unveils her eye,
In tranquil sleep the world shall lie,
    And serf and king like blessings share;
'Tis then thy voice in music falls
Along my heart's deserted halls,
   Whose mould'ring rafters find their guest
     Too sweet to bear.

MY BLIND CANARY.

Who made thy song so all divine,
    My blind canary?
Who taught thy little tongue to sing?
Who gave thy voice a heavenly ring?
    How learned thee thus to sweetly vary
The long vibrations of thy muse,
And o'er high angels to diffuse
    A lay too fine for hearts like mine,
      So sad and weary?

What dark-wing'd fate close-sealed thine eyes,
    My soul's enchanter?
A fate, maybe, of high decree
Ordained this world thou shouldst not see,
    Or that our life's a cheat and banter.
The heart's deep wrong, the maiden's tear,
The pain, the strife, suspense and fear;—
    Our woes to know thou art too wise.
      Sweet heaven haunter.

Dost sing the joys of warmer climes,
    My little stranger?

Those changeless green Canary Isles,
Where ever long the summer smiles
    On tamarin and forest ranger?
On those green isles, lapped by the sea,
Perennial blooms thy parent tree,
    Far from man's sins, far from his crimes,
    And far from danger.

How came thee from thy sunny isles,
    In cold to wander?
As poets from the heavens are flung
Poor mortals of this earth among,
    For bread to sing, and starve, and pander,
Thou minstrel of the stately palms,
In frosty climes doth sing for alms,
    Where man beguiles with heartless wiles,
    Deceit and slander.

The yucca and the citron tree
    Thou knowest no more;
The guavas sweet and mangosteen
Will never more by thee be seen;
    Thy treble note no more will pour

O'er mango, palm and asphodel,
And pomegranate, and aureate beil;
   No more, my bird, thy vision's free
      To see thy native shore.

   There is a morn of brighter beams
      Thine eyes beneath,
Than ever shone to mortal view,
Or fancy's painting ever drew;
   Thy downy form is but the sheath,
And music, flashing on its throne
Of paradise and burnished zone,
   Thy world illumes, and incense teems
      On thy laurel wreath.

   When low the plume of awful Death
      In dusk descends
Upon the couch where life is run,
And cold oblivion's night begun,
   Ere yet the soul its casement rends,
The lights of heaven pass in review,
And waning hopes their pulse renew:

Such scenes are thine, to which thy breath
   Its sweetness lends.

O ! minstrel of the mystic trill,
   And rhyme elastic !
There is a singer in my breast
That rises to thy vocal crest,
   Though long her lute has lain monastic;
Thy dulcet notes with thee she'd share,
But since thy song's untinged with care,
   She stoops, and droops, and wanders still
     Amid her dreams dynastic.

I dwell in space and nothingness;
   With thee I'd soar !
I live in echoes of the past,
Which from the grave are to me cast,
   Like phantoms on the midnight shore.
When hope would come, a weight is here,
Which crushes pride, yet bridles fear;
   For hope's misgivings bring distress
     None can explore.

To thy far heights with thee I'd rise,
    With soul unchained;
To that domain beyond the sky,
Beyond the clouds that on me lie,
    Beyond what thought has e'er attained.
O! there falls a sheen of golden light,
Chasing away the pensive night;
    It blends with rays of milder glow
    And bears me from this world below,
        Till faith's maintained.

THE COBBLER.

IN cellar close and drear and dark,
   Beneath the sidewalk low,
I see the cobbler's busy hands,
   I see his steady blow.
His body's bent upon his last,
   His lamp hangs on the wall,
And in and out he whips his ends,
   And plies his nimble awl.
      Tip tap, from sun to sun;
      Tip tap, the night's begun,
      And he has work that must be done;
         Tip tap.

His apron's spread across his breast,
   Of leathern texture strong;
His arms are bare, his sleeves rolled up;
   His feet brace tight the thong,

Which binds the last between his knees;
  His pull is swift and long:
And now the pegs he hammers in,
  Humming a little song.
    Tip tap, from sun to sun;
    Tip tap, the night's begun,
    And he has work that must be done;
      Tip tap.

For evening chat, a crony plods
  Adown the creaking stair;
He naively cracks a rustic joke,
  And forward draws his chair.
At wit the cobbler tries his skill,
  The friendly joke to floor:
In sounding words he makes retort,
  And both in chorus roar.

The current news is now discussed—
  What men have said or done;
And how they erred in this or that,
  And where they honor won.

(The best and fairest he will be,
　Of whom it can be said :
He worked to give a fellow-man
　A way to earn his bread.
Much closer to the human breast
　Than all of glory's store,
Will be the simple words : " He found
　Employment for the poor.")

With elbows placed upon his knees,
　And fingers raised to show
The nice deductions of his mind,
　The cobbler's reasons flow ;
And then he pegs and pegs away,
　He knows the minutes speed ;
His work's behind the promised time,
　And he has mouths to feed.
　　Tip tap, from sun to sun ;
　　Tip tap, the night's begun,
　　　And he has work that must be done ;
　　　　Tip tap.

Now sound befogs the lines of sense,
    And, full of wisdom's pride,
On reason's back he rolls a weight,
    Which reason will not ride;
But down all in the dust she lies,
    Dust of an empty head,
And kicks her heels against his tongue,
    'Till his kind face is red.

Feeling a pain that he has erred,
    He stops where pride begins,
And, holding out his manly hand,
    He shows how goodness wins;
The palms are joined in kindly grasp,
    Contending words are o'er,
And in that lock of cordial love,
    True friendship they restore.

Now, fumbling through his kit, he finds
    That solace to his care—
That balm between two cronies dear—
    The pipe, which both may share.

The smoke now curls above his head,
    From smacks both loud and full;
Then with his thumb the shank he wipes,
    With "Jim, now, take a pull."

He nods with pleasure to the wall,
    Where mended boots are hung;
He points to those that great men own,
    Whose fame has long been sung.
To vamp the boot that honor wears
    Is fame enough for him;
Content is he to labor on,
    Until his eyes grow dim.

Despise him not, ye rich and vain;
    He has a father's care:
His boys and girls to clothe and feed,
    A wife his bread to share.
Beneath his rough and homely garb,
    A manly heart and true
Beats warm with all a father's love,
    And all that love can do.

THE COBBLER.

The pride of wealth is not for him,
    Still less the pride of fame ;
They are the thieves that rob the heart,
    To gain an empty name.
With sky above and earth beneath,
    His Eden floats between ;
And life is bliss, when pride and state
    Are not with envy seen.

Some day, ere yet the sun is up,
    Or ere the sun goes down,
The crape will hang upon his door,
    Unnoticed by the town.
Like shadows will his patrons pass,
    And turn their gaze away,
For friendship dies between our sighs,
    When friends return to clay.

Eternity shall guard his dust
    When monuments shall fall,
And clouds, the breathing of the moon,
    Shall myriad time recall.

A man was he of artless ways,
    To Nature always true ;
He ne'er assumed what he was not,
    But lived for what he knew.

THERE IS A BRIGHT SPOT IN THE SKY.

THE dream of years ofttimes betrays
A golden grief over golden days—
A grief which chants, on memory's shell,
The requiem of a dead farewell;
But when its strains grow low and die,
There is a bright spot in the sky.

With all life's ills I am content,
If well my days are daily spent.
When phantoms from a distant land,
Shall come and lead me by the hand,
Resigned I'll go, without a sigh,
For there's a bright spot in the sky.

Should hearts grow cold and men forget
The hand that placed them in its debt,
Since error is the fate of all,
And some will stand, while some will fall,

No man by me shall prostrate lie,
While there's a bright spot in the sky.

This world is good to him that lives
Within the bounds that nature gives;
But roses bloom and roses fade,
And brightest jewels have their shade;
If gloom surround, then gaze on high,
And find a bright spot in the sky.

In every home let sunshine dwell,
On every face let kindness tell,
In every heart let peace find rest,
And should pale sorrow wring the breast,
Take courage then, and look on high;
There's still a bright spot in the sky.

To other hearts and other hands,
To other climes and other lands,
The coast is dark along that main
Whose pilgrims ne'er return again;
But in that long and last good-bye,
A star will guide from sky to sky.

IN YONDER VALE.

IN yonder vale there is a lowly mound,
　　Where sleeps forever all I ever found,
In this strange world of phantom and disguise,
To give my soul a glimpse of Paradise.

She came to me ere love was known to death,
When joy expanded on the south wind's breath;
An angel of sweetness, strayed from Heaven's choir,
To light my soul with love's divinest fire.

I tire of love's graces now. She is dead;
The air rests heavy on me as of lead;
Ere yet my days have reached their sunny prime,
I totter on the crutch of crumbling time.

When beauty roves along yon silent vale,
And reads in flowers the gentle lover's tale,
This low-pulsed music then will close around—
Our deepest sorrow to dead love is bound.

AUTUMN LEAVES.

'TIS now the hour when rays decline
On withered leaf and broken vine,
When birds fly homeward from the hill,
And leaves drop darkly on the sill.
O leaves, that vernal days recall,
Why do you fall—why do you fall?

Across the woof of dusk and shade
The tawny elves disport and fade:
While whispers, swathed in love's command,
Would lure me hence to fairy land.
O leaves, that dear old friends recall,
Why do you fall—why do you fall?

The moaning winds bring thoughts to me
As lonely as the leafless tree;
Like autumn leaves, my day is passed,
And pathless night is overcast.
O leaves, that life's proud hopes recall,
Why do you fall—why do you fall?

I know, alas!—now that I'm old—
To me the world is strange and cold.
What by-gone joys it will renew
To join my friends beyond the blue!
O leaves, that bosom friends recall,
Why do you fall—why do you fall?

Come, silent death, and take your fee,
For it is something to be free—
An element of sky and sea
In boundless immortality.
O leaves, that dreams of heaven recall,
Why do you fall—why do you fall?

Ah, joys of youth and tears of age,
There never yet was priest or sage
That could return without regret
To where his youth and manhood met.
Shrines on my head the dead leaves fall,
And my soul whispers: "God is all."

TAKE BACK THE RING.

TAKE back the ring thy finger wore,
   It ne'er shall circle mine;
Take back the ring; I'll trust no more
   A heart so false as thine.

The love which closed in blissful sleep,
   To dream of heaven and thee,
Awakes to know, but not to weep,
   How false thy vows can be.

No grief shall wring my trusting breast,
   No pain my heart shall know;
In gentle peace my soul shall rest;
   No tear for thee shall flow.

The heart that wins a morning love,
   To evening loves incline;
As stars engage us from above,
   When meteors round us shine.

Fresh hopes to cheer, thy way is clear,
    'Tis lit with flick'ring joy:
Return to her, to thee so dear,
    Nor her sweet peace destroy.

Take back the ring thy finger wore,
    It ne'er shall sully mine;
I loved thee once; I plight no more
    At thy unhallowed shrine.

THE EDITOR'S GRAVE.

THE sward was damp with falling dew,
    The moaning wind around me blew,
And sadly came, from wood and glade,
A dirge for him so lowly laid.

The vault let down its sombre gray,
Night turned her key upon the day,
And, near and far, on moving mote,
My dreamy sorrow seemed to float.

As floats the soul when death is near,
And pulse is low with ebbing fear,
So sped my life at every breath,
Which closer drew me into death.

As weeping makes the soul divine,
My spirit rose from its decline,
And lay, above my tears, at rest,
By chastening sadness calm and blest.

THE EDITOR'S GRAVE.

Ere yet the shades obscured my view,
And round him Gloom his mantle drew,
Upon the West's entombing roll
I traced the embers of his soul;

And in the tinges mingling there,
I saw Life's contest with Despair,
And, in the last dissolving ray,
One noble spirit fade away.

The sun, the glory—all is past,
And buried in the depths at last.
What recks it now, his labor done,
The garlands he had lost or won?

By honor and by conscience led,
Truth's halo glowed around his head,
And filled his pen with golden light,
To brand the wrong and gem the right.

On a world's pulse he laid his hand,
By every clime his thoughts were fanned;
The fibrils of his jewelled mind
Were strained in glory for his kind.

THE EDITOR'S GRAVE.

Oft rising high to God, his King,
    Heaven's bending arch he made his bow,
The lightning's flash his pliant string,
    And sprung his thunder at the foe.

Against the wrong his touch was keen,
Yet bore no trace of vulgar spleen;
He ne'er in rage his weapon broke;
The touch was stronger than the stroke.

Obscure in toil, cheated of fame,
He loved his labor all the same;
He knew, whate'er that labor cost,
In life or death there's nothing lost.

Here lies the poor neglected scribe,
Whom no man's purse could ever bribe;
His crown of glory was his trust;
His dust now mingles with the just;

And from it forth the rose shall spring,
And through that rose the zephyrs sing;
And o'er it rest an angel's boon,
As calm as grave beneath the moon.

I SHALL RISE WITH THE LARK.

 SHALL rise with the lark at the break of the morn,
With a garland of hope that the day shall adorn;
And from angels above joyful rays shall descend,
With the bloom of my spirit their lustre to blend.

From the rise of the sun to the wane of its flame,
I shall find my true praise in the lisp of my name
By the child-lips I love; and, whatever betide,
I shall keep my heart warm for my own fireside.

Fair friendship may greet me, as forward I go,
And fame, for the moment, its guerdon bestow;
But the smiles of my babes are more dear to my soul
Than all that the world or its splendors control.

As the rays of the sun are the light of the earth,
The eyes of my darlings are the joy of my earth;
As the zephyrs at eve breathe balm to the bowers,
Sweet songs through my halls shed the perfume of
 flowers.

Their salvos of joy, giving strength to my will,
O'er the trials of life, are encouragement still;
Nor sorrow, nor torment, with me shall abide,
While I keep my heart warm for my own fireside.

Should my fair rose of morning at evening decay,
And the star that I followed decline with the day,
I'il turn from a world which is mournfully wide,
With a heart that beats warm for my own fireside.

Let home-love, and peace, and contentment be mine,
While the revel I shun, and the quicksands of wine;—
Let me think of the mother who once was my bride,
'Till I glow with the charm of my own fireside.

THE GHOST OF CASTLE MORR.

PROUD Castle Morr, above the lake,
    For centuries stood in solemn gray,
And round its brow the thorn and brake,
    Entwined and trailed, as chaplets lay.

From cliff and tower the eye might range
    Along the breast of Scotia's Isle,
And view, amidst no cosmos change,
    The shaft of many a ruined pile.

Lord MELMONT, proud of blood and name,
    Was master long of Castle Morr,
And grandees to his banquets came
    From sultry Ind and frigid Nor'.

The lights were lit in MELMONT's halls,
    As evening June had veiled her head;
And proudly shone along the walls
    The symbols of the glorious dead.

The shield, the mace, the mail were there,
    The javelin, bow, the swinging glave;
And plaided clans, with strong limbs bare,
    Smiled, from their portraits, on the brave.

The banquet spread, the gallant guest
    Is bowed to place around the board;
The bow's returned with lofty crest,
    And manner grave, and civil word.

And fairest dames of high degree,
    With melting love upon their lips,
And shoulders bare, and bosoms free,
    Advance with smiles and coyish slips.

And DORAH sweet, the nuptial bride,
    With curving neck and regal head,
In all the wealth of beauty's pride,
    By bowing valor forth is led.

The banquet o'er, the song went round:
    The knights sang praise of woman's love;
The ladies, by nice favor bound,
    Sang Scotia's lords high over Jove.

Now, why doth MELMONT's face grow pale,
　　On this his eve of marriage vows?
What low, sweet voice floats on the gale?
　　What sudden pain contracts his brows?

A soldier proud was MELMONT brave,
　　Whose valiant deeds on India's plains
Sent foes in legions to their grave,
　　And gave a peace to broad domains.

When battle raised its rueful head,
　　With waving plume and sabre bright,
On champing steed bold MELMONT led,
　　With Princess SAHLA at his right.

When "Charge the foe!" he gave command,
　　And quick and thick the missiles flew,
Fair SAHLA waved her dauntless hand,
　　And from her zone her weapon drew.

She fought two battles locked in one:
　　While courage swept her to the foe,
To spur and cheer her troopers on,
　　Her love engaged her lover's woe.

Pale, sunk with fear, she saw the bolts
  That rang in air round MELMONT's head,
And all her prowess met revolts
  In sudden darts of love and dread.

Nor laggard shown in MELMONT's love :
  Behind the window of his thought,
And fierce resolve his name to prove,
  Affection's web love's weaver wrought.

Oh, heavy day! Oh, luckless charge
  That bore fair SAHLA to the van,
Where, fighting on the battle's marge,
  She captive fell to Hindostan !

What doom awaits this lover true,
  Who fled her rajah's royal halls,
And from a Scottish chieftain drew
  That love whose thraldom disenthralls ?

Deep passion now was mixed with pain
  In MELMONT's ardent, raging breast ;
But well the soldier could restrain
  All outward sign of rude unrest.

The Brahmin plot and Hindoo skill
    Returned the Princess to her sire,
Whose kindly breast o'er captious will
    Could never of affection tire.

As fancy's lamp pursues the light
    That floats around in fiction's mind,
Through gleamings slight of hope in night
    His love sad MELMONT seeks to find.

He storms the shaman priest's retreat,
    He storms the rajah's frowning wall;
He's everywhere, with flying feet,
    And bulwarks echo at his call.

Within, without, beyond the bounds
    Of priest's and rajah's stern control,
Swift vanished hopes and hollow sounds
    Are all that reach sad MELMONT's soul.

Now ten long years their tides have rolled
    Since India's air his brow had fanned—
Since SAHLA sweet and MELMONT bold
    Their love and life had pledged and planned.

And now that voice again is heard,
   Despite of friends, despite of foes,
That won the heart of Scotland's laird
   Along Himmaleh's broad plateaus.

She sings the song he loved to hear
   Below the stars, when winds were still,
When from the heart there swelled a tear,
   Which rose and fell at music's trill.

A gem illumes his searching eye—
   The ring he gave her with a kiss,
When love, like waves, rolled mountain high,
   And all the world was vales of bliss.

Now darker shades rise on the wall,
   And whispered words, in lighter tone,
Conjecture forms, and keenly fall
   On fears that all dislike to own.

All sadly from the banquet rose
   The noble host of Castle Morr;
And his proud heart seemed full of woes,
   Which none divined the reason for.

Now hurried looks meet anxious eyes,
  And Sahla's calm and gentle mien
The scrutiny of all defies
  Of who she is or who has been.

Her olive hands and olive face,
  Her liquid eyes of Orient hue,
Her gliding step and languid grace,
  Where'er she moved could all subdue.

She quits the hall with gentle ways,
  And follows fast in Melmont's wake;
While jealousy the bride betrays,
  And speechless hurries to the lake.

The kinsman of the noble bride,
  At Melmont's conduct sore enraged,
Now flash their dress-swords from their side,
  And hot in converse stand engaged.

Their words are few, indignant, strong;
  From what they heard and what they saw
Of Dorah's grief and Melmont's wrong,
  Suspicion feeds on lines they draw.

Enough! enough! Revenge is near!
  Through lawn and bower and vista fair
The pride-stung nobles search and steer,
  But find not MELMONT anywhere.

There is a room in Castle Morr,
  A secret chamber, quaint and grand,
Which few e'er knew the service for,
  Save he whose word was in command.

To shield her from undue reproof
  By tongues unruly, sharp and free,
There SAHLA's placed, from all aloof,
  And cautious MELMONT turns the key.

Now from the window where she sits
  The Princess muses on the night;
While shadow after shadow flits
  By fern and fir, within her sight.

For MELMONT's life those shadows seek,
  And for his life he boldly stands,
In calm defense prepared to speak,
  And fairly meet all fair demands.

But passion rules the omened hour,
   And fury strikes him to the ground :
Which SAHLA sees from yonder tower,
   And breaks her heart-strings at a bound.

Now pity's tongue the tale will tell,
   How gentle hands, unknown to fame,
Had set a plant where MELMONT fell,
   And called it by that hero's name.

E'er since that hour, at midnight tide,
   A curtain of the blackest lace
On windowed Morr is drawn aside,
   Disclosing there a pallid face.

It looks a minute down the lake
   It glances round in secret pain,
As if it feared some foe awake ;
   And then the curtain's drawn again.

For eons folk have come to see,
   O'er hill and dale and jagged tor,
The DORAH lake, the MELMONT tree,
   And SAHLA's ghost at Castle Morr.

A FEW BRIEF YEARS.

A FEW brief years and I shall lie
　　Beneath yon calm and peaceful sky,
Whose breast is bright with notes and bars,
And laughing music of the stars,—
Whose bosom, spread from pole to pole,
In silence will my grave console.

With straightened limbs my shade will rest,
My head against my coffin pressed;
And hour by hour, and day by day,
My vapored dust will pass away.

This hand that writes will then be cold,
And shrunk and eaten with the mold
Of time and death and dark decay,
Till joint by joint returns to clay.

The dread, the fear, the torment sore,
Will rend my heart-strings never more,
Nor human wiles nor worldly strife,
To barely win the bread of life,
Will ne'er, within my narrow bed,
Disturb or wake my wearied head.

A thousand years will pass me by,
Without a change in land or sky;
Nor winter's snow, nor summer's heat,
Will e'er disturb my winding sheet.

At evening's close I'll meet no more
The smile that waits me at the door;
The hills and dales and streams will be
A mute forevermore to me.

No morn will wake me at its dawn;
No more, on mead or field or lawn,
When landscapes smile beneath the sun,
Will romping childhood to me run.

O happy day, these eyes will close
To life's contentions and its woes,
And all the miseries that ban
The mystic course of foolish man.

My span of life, my humble lot,
Like friendship's vows, will be forgot;
And all the world will live the same
As if I never had a name.

CONTEMPLATION.

THE bright waves leap
    Across the steep,
And in the deep are lost forever;
    If I must sing,
    My hopes take wing
Through shades of gloom, returning never.

    Oh soul opprest!
    Where is that rest
For which I crave, and pine, and sorrow?
    Where is that beam
    That, in a dream,
Forever shines but for to-morrow?

    The fiends of air
    And spectres bare
Lay cold and withered hands upon me;
    And joy's sweet sound
    Goes round and round,
Beyond my reach, to mock and shun me.

CONTEMPLATION.

Does my God know
The weight of woe
I daily, hourly suffer under?
Are hearts opprest
Ne'er to be blest
Till every chord is rent asunder?

This cold, sad earth
Gave me not birth,
For all around is strange and gloomy;
The eyes I meet
I fear to greet,
For in the air there's danger to me.

The words of men
Affright me when
In moods my spirit soars above me;
And oft I try
To crush a sigh
For those I love—for those that love me.

From main to main
The world's wild strain
Is painful to my wakeful senses;

And in my blood
There is a flood
That down would sweep on man's offenses.

My star is set,
My eyelids wet;
Upon me falls the night eternal;
My struggling breath,
Half born of death,
The soul would free from chains infernal.

Oh star of night!
Why shine so bright,
Since far I am from thy proud splendor?
Why mock my gloom
My living tomb,
With dreams that die in doubt and wonder?

Do thy pure beams,
That fill my dreams,
And lead me up to realms supernal,

CONTEMPLATION.

Do they, O star,
Shoot wide and far
Into all space that is nocturnal?

Far, far away,
On tombstones gray,
Oblivion drear thy light creeps over;
Dark, sad and prone,
Crushed, bound, alone,
Around thee still my soul must hover.

My thoughts I turn
To thoughts that burn
And tremble and glow, to seize the proof
And reason why
I live to die;
But reason and proof stand far aloof.

I move along
With life's dull throng,
Wrapt in the mysteries of the world;

CONTEMPLATION.

The more I climb
To realms sublime,
My soul from heaven is deeper hurled.

In souls a-lull,
The light burns dull;
Nor fires consume the peaceful breast;
But thoughts at strife
With this dark life
Supply the flames that never rest.

I turn the eye,
And wonder why
Cities are built and toil is endless;
I look aghast
At swift years past:
Cities are dead, and graves are friendless.

Oh weary soul!
Where is the goal
For which you long and pine and sorrow?

Where is the star
That shines afar,
And cheats you ever in the morrow?

If man is born
This world to scorn,
And still to give the senses ease,
Some sphere above,
Some realm of love
Must all his hopes at last appease.

OH, WEARY COMES THE NIGHT.

OH, weary comes the night,
    But sadder still the morn,
For who would see the light
    With love that is forlorn?

Then die, poor lingering flame,
    For who would suffer under
The mocking of love's name
    When hearts are rent asunder?

And should my memory wake,
    Love's last fond look revealing,
Let death the mirror break,
    Its joy and woe concealing.

Oh, who can bear the pangs,
    When love, unfettered, soaring,
On barb and breaker hangs,
    The sweets of life outpouring?

Ah, me, to feel love's pain
    Through love its chambers creeping!
Like sunbeams in the rain,
    Love shines while I am weeping.

TO HER SPIRIT.

A LITTLE bird flies out of my heart,
   A bird all white as snow;
And I am sad for the void she leaves,
   A void none else can know.

Into the gloom she takes her way;
   My eyes grow dim with grief;
Broken the shell, empty the nest,
   And faith deserts belief.

I call to my bird to come back to me,
   But a raven comes instead;
And over my soul he seeks control,
   And on my breast his bed.

Far up in yon cloud a rift I see—
   I see my love go through,
On angel wings, in a halo divine,
   That God alone should view.

A LOVE THOUGHT.

LOVELY, sweet, and gentle maiden,
    How fares thy heart with mine?
Lovely, sweet, and gentle maiden,
  Fairest star in fairest Aiden,
    Oh, dost thou know I pine?

Bright diamond of Love's morning dew,
    There is no place so fair
To holy love and joyful eyes,
And sacred thoughts and sacred sighs,
    As by the Delaware.

The lily beats against my breast,
    And I the balm inhale;
But as I reach to pluck the rose,
Around the gem the petals close,
    And my poor efforts fail.

A LOVE THOUGHT.

On me, from thy celestial glow,
    Descends the trembling ray;
But as I would that ray control,
And light the chambers of my soul,
    It fades—it fades away.

Come, zephyrs, from my love afar,
    Come, solace to my care;
Oh, ne'er through perfumed garden strayed
A more redolent budding maid
    Than the lass of Delaware.

MY DOLLIE.

WHAT is my sorrow to others?
    Who weeps, my Dollie, for you?
'Tis more than the grief of a mother's
    That pierces me through and through.

Strangled you lay before me,
    Strangled by cruel death,
Before one thought came o'er me
    That you were robbed of breath.

You were to me my morning,
    Before my toil begun,
I in your beauty scorning
    All toil beneath the sun.

My angel, I loved you dearly,
    No tongue can utter my woe;
My angel, I loved you dearly,
    With a love that angels know.

MY DOLLIE.

You're gone forever, my darling,
    And I can find no rest ;
You're gone forever, my darling,
    And left me a bleeding breast.

Your eyes were bright, my beauty,
    And large and sweet and brown ;
Your eyes were bright, my beauty,
    With lashes drooping down.

I knew your talk was simple,
    And I saw, when you'd begin,
The playing of the dimple
    On little cheek and chin.

Oh, for a day of life again !
    Oh, for an hour to love you !
My wretched heart will break with pain
    To see the sod above you.

O snow, be kind to Dollie,
    She, tossed you on her hair ;
O rose be kind to Dollie,
    For she was sweet and fair.

MY DOLLIE.

Weary and sad my soul is gone,
  In spirit land to find you,
While in my arms, O cherished one,
  Unto my breast I bind you.

In my tearful, bitter sorrow,
  Hope looks trembling to the day;
Yet from grief I solace borrow
  That an angel leads the way.

THE VETERAN.

I SAW him at the bar,
   He had a pretty star
      On his breast;
His nose was ruby red,
With pimple somewhat spread
      As a guest.

Of beard his face was bare,
Except a tuft of hair
      On his lip;
It shall not be denied
That little tuft was dyed
      On the tip.

He showed a rounded waist,
With shoulders tightly braced,
      Militaire,

His manners were polite,
His breeding always right,
    To a hair.

When he was sound in health,
On 'Change he made his wealth,
    Like a wink;
But the money he had lent,
And the way his shekels went,
    Made him drink.

His relatives were rich,
But then there was a hitch—
    He had brain;
His friends would save and hoard,
While he his ducats poured
    Out like rain.

It gave him greater pleasure
To talk about the treasure
    Of a friend,

Than if he a check could fill
For a million at his will,
    Just to spend.

He held knowledge by the roots,
And could settle all disputes
    With a smile ;
And the wisdom in his looks
Showed he swallowed mighty books
    By the pile.

Tomes were not his special fort,
He was scienced as a sport,
    And could name,
In the dark, to hear him patter,
Any dog, from bull to ratter,
    That was game.

Whether sound and swift and true,
By his joints a horse he knew,
    And his source ;

Nags he saw, of no great shakes,
Often win the biggest stakes
  On the course.

Once crossed he was in love,
She was a pretty dove—
  Without mind;
And she chose to make her bed
With a coarse vermilion head—
  Went it blind.

His name was Baxter Blum,
He was a healthy plum—
  Such a nose!
With a forehead like an ape's,
And a shape for bows and scrapes,
  Kicks and blows.

Blum was, alas! her choice—
She had a lovely voice,
  And could sing;

But no one can find out
Why love will skip about—
  Just to sting.

His life was one of fate,
He took his whiskey straight—
  Never squealed ;
But vowed by valiant Hector
That genius loved her nectar
  Till she reeled.

He had his day of riches,
But now his seedy breeches
  Made him wise ;
He was so near the dumping,
Prepared he was for jumping—
  To the skies.

His heels were bare of hose,
And peeping were his toes
  Through his shoes ;

THE VETERAN.

Gincocktails were his trouble,
And up they bent him double,
   For a snooze.

He then showed off in snoring,
Till he was voted boring,
   All in state;
The last he's heard to mutter:
" I'm swept into the gutter!
   Such is fate!"

MISS NIGHT.

MISS Night she is a winsome lass,
    And dresses with a tidy care:
The moon she makes her looking-glass,
    And with the stars she braids her hair.

She frolics over Juno's bars,
    With silence in her hidden hand;
And then she laughs, and flings her stars
    At every lover in the land.

She dips her dark limbs in the sea;
    Above the cloud her face is hid;
Against the wind she bends her knee,
    While seated on Aurora's lid.

The broad expanse is her domain,
    Her pinnace is the scudding gale;
Restraining which she sets a chain
    Of dappling waves against her sail.

Behind the gauze that floats between
    Her gown of black and hood of gray,
What would be seen remains unseen,
    And passes to a brighter day.

And thus the light that follows hope,
    Our doubtings veil it from the eye;
And here in darkness man must grope,
    Since light of faith's beyond the sky.

SPEAK TRUTH.

SPEAK truth and sense, or silent still remain,
Nor edge your words to give your neighbor pain.
By honest art must man for man be used;
By brutish man is only man abused.

Before you speak, be satisfied the soul
Is in full sympathy and full control;
Temper too oft the thoughtless voice succeeds,
And shames the soul by wrong and foolish deeds.
Wild are the words that on mad passion fly;
Like sparks they're uttered, and like sparks they die.

THE COMMUNIST.

THAT wealth is stealth is now the cry,
    And rogues are they that keep it;
And he's a knave who'd plot and try
    To raise and hoard and heap it.

His house or bed, his coat or hat,
    He should assign or lend it;
What right has he to this or that,
    If he can not defend it?

The right of one is right of all,
    The learned tramp well knows it:
If with a blow the rich must fall,
    The sportive wight bestows it.

When fever maddens in the veins,
    We soothe and cheat and nurse it;
'Twould only aggravate our pains
    To rage and rave and curse it.

But mortals make the error strange,
    To right a wrong, misuse it;
It is within true wisdom's range,
    Its life is to abuse it.

From end to end this land is free
    To those who would enjoy it;
And he's a knave of low degree
    Who'd labor to destroy it.

He's but a slave who would complain,
    With hands and health to lift him;
For patient work will comfort gain,
    And forward ever shift him.

Know this, ye men of sloth and woe,
    And to your faith ye pin it:
The rank of him is never low
    Who has the brain to win it.

A day will tell the ail of life,
    There's nothing for to-morrow;
'Tis mind that suffers in the strife,
    And bears the weight of sorrow.

LINES TO A FRIEND.

MY heart is sad to-night, my friend,
   And I am bent with care;
The sorrows that with memories blend,
   Make life too hard to bear.

I had my day! I ran my race!
   My life is aimless now;
And all its woes my fingers trace
   In furrows on my brow.

Old friends are dead, or scattered wide,
   Across the world's domain;
Nor day nor night, nor time nor tide,
   Will bring them back again.

My dreams of youth—long past and gone—
   I would not now recall;
For time has made me old and wan,
   And I but wait my fall.

LINES TO A FRIEND.

No tears shall damp my faded cheek.
   No joy shall fill my breast;
This world has naught that I would seek.
   I only long for rest.

KINGS ARE MADE BY SLAVES.

MEN of living thought, awake!
    Men of will and brain and nerve!
Chains which gall your freedom, break!
    Scorn the hands a despot serve!
Let the voice of Freedom ring:
Only slaves can make a king.

Man was born of Nature's God,
    Not a thing, at tyrant's call,
Not a crouching, fawning clod,
    Asking leave to lick and crawl.
Let insulted manhood vow:
None but slaves to despots bow.

Come you from a slavish land,
    Where to king you bent the knee?
Touch not, serf, a freeman's hand,
    Till repentance makes you free.

He's a slave in heart and soul
Who will suffer king's control.

Where's the vigor of your blood,
    Crouching, cringing, fawning dog?
Are your veins but sluggish mud?
    Is your head a brainless log?
Let the cry of freemen ring:
Dogs alone obey a king.

See yon slave in want and rags!
    See him cower and bare the head,
As his brazen despot wags,
    Struts and shakes, with pompous tread.
Weep, O Manhood, at the sight!
Serfdom base, and ravished right!

God of Patience! see the slaves
    Marshalled forth in bold array,
Bearing arms to fight for knaves!
    Murd'ring men for hireling pay!
Hear the air with God's voice ring:
"None but slaves can make a king."

To perdition, one and all!
    Hell was made for crown and king!
Downward, hellward, let them fall!
    On their thrones let bullets ring!
Be the freeman's watchword still:
"Tyrants I'm ordained to kill."

Strike the dagger to his heart!
    Let the crimson life-blood flow!
Do not shudder, do not start;
    It is Freedom's proudest blow.
Let the cry of manhood ring:
Dog is he who serves a king.

What you are let tyrants know;
    Do not act the craven slave;
Stamp your mettle with a blow
    On the head of kingly knave.
Be whatever else you can,
But, for Christ's sake! be a MAN!

THE FIRE.

HARK!—that knell!
What means that bell?—
That rousing swell?
It dies, it sinks in parted links.

Again it thrills! Again it fills!
Waking, shaking, leaping higher,
In a flaming tongue of fire.

See the smoke! See the cloud!
Darker, denser, wider growing,
Rising, falling, sweeping, blowing.

Swift and eager come the crowd,
Rushing, pushing, shouting, yelling,
Love to save, each bosom swelling—
  Swelling, swelling, swelling!

THE FIRE.

Place the engine! Seize the hose!
Let the water boldly float
On the fiendish fiery foes,
And the engine puff her throat.

Oh, the flames! Oh, the flames!
Winding, wafting, twisting, turning,
Cracking, scorching, blazing, burning!
    Burning, burning, burning!

Hear those names! Hear those claims!
Save me, father! Save me, mother!
Sister, save me! Save me, brother!

Raise the stream! Raise the stream!
Love and life are sinking, failing,
Midst seas of flame there's loud bewailing,
Whilst daring hearts the walls are scaling,
    Scaling, scaling, scaling!

Hark, that cry! Hear that sigh!
Oh, that scream! Horrors teem!
Mailed in might, stout hearts are wielding
Axes bright, from danger shielding
Life's last throbs nigh before they die.

THE FIRE.

Oh, the clashing! oh, the crashing!
Madly rising, tearing, dashing,
Wildly flouncing, flaring, flashing,
Red flames lash the broken sash.

Hark, hark, within—a breath, a din!
Groaning, moaning, clinging, grasping,
Life on fire, a fireman clasping!
Clasping, clasping, clasping!

Now, now you see the flames are free!
Spouting, spreading, waving, soaring,
Plunging, tossing, raging, roaring,
In one hot sea of dread decree.

The high-raised throws from spurting hose,
Tending, bending, warping, winding,
Seeking, chasing, meeting, blinding
Each blast that blows from fiery foes.

O God, that wall! That prayer, that fall!
Ruin, wreck, and desolation,
Ravage, waste, and devastation,
Spread Death's sad pall dark over all.

THE FIRE.

Was it a beam, or brick, or stone
Tore here the flesh, broke there a bone?
Matted and moiled, floats here and there,
Clotted with blood, a tuft of hair.

Look on that head! See where the beam
Bared to the scalp, and round the seam,
Uprooted, loose, flying away,
Hair by hair, wherever it may.

That lurid glare! That ghastly stare!
Bruised, maimed, and gashed, soiled, stained,
 and broken,
Of former looks scarce left a token.

Could those lips speak, how they could tell
Of direful woe and fortune fell!
For mother's grief those eyes have shed;
For brother's pain that still heart bled.

As on that shattered form I gaze,
Where deepening gloom emits its rays,
Where life might linger, yet is not,
I waver in man's future lot.

On that brow a thought is molded,
On those lips a word lies folded;
Immortal word—immortal thought!
What seraph fleet the whisper caught?

What now is light or gloom, or earth or air,
To that wild stare?
Or friend or foe, or joy or woe,
Or frown or smile, or trust or guile,
To that dead glare?
Peace rests but in the tomb.

THE CONEY ISLAND TRACK.

ROUND the Coney Island track
Many a racer stretched his back,
Many a dollar lost and won,
Since the season first begun.

Gallant men and ladies fair
Met and laughed and mingled there;
On the benches, light as cork,
Sat the darlings of New York;
Posing in his beauty by
Smirked the nobby cuss, so fly;
Gathered near, in hodden-gray,
Stared the coots of Sheepshead bay;
And the Gravesend sturgeon bet
All the product of his net:

THE CONEY ISLAND TRACK.

While the zephyrs from the sea
Music sang in every tree.

Now the start is just at hand,
And the judges take their stand—
To their noses tip their hats,
Blink around like furtive cats.
Eye the sun with sober wink,
Raise the jug and take a drink,
Draw their watches, look at time,
Hum some words of sporting rhyme,
Place their lorgnettes to their eyes,
Gaze about, in sweet surprise,
At the ladies and their plumes,
At the horses and their grooms,
At the bubbles sailing gay
Over track and far away.

As they caper to and fro,
Every eye the flyers know
By the jockey's black or blue,
Green or red or yellow hue.

Striped like zebras, on the track
Tomtits hold their chargers back,
While they wait, away to pop
When the flags the starters drop.

What excitement! O, what fun!
Neck and neck the racers run!
Round the track they shoot and fly,
Like winged devils from the sky.
Now they turn and wheel and bend,
Now they merge and mix and blend,
Till it gives the eye the itch
To discover which is which.

Now the brown and now the gray,
Whirling, flying, leads the way;
Now the sorrel, now the black
Leads the leader in the rack.
Riders far their bodies strain
To each charger's flying mane,
Madly blending their desire
With the racer's rage and fire.

THE CONEY ISLAND TRACK.

To the goal the victor reels,
Flinging time from flying heels.
Loud hurrahs and waving hats,
And the ladies' petty-pats
With their dainty gloves, so fine,
Hail the winner on the line.

Bets are off, and bets are on,
Some have lost, and some have won,
But they all have had their fun,
For the track fills beauty's eye,
And they leave it with a sigh,
Slowly wending to their home,
Singing glory to JEROME.

FRIENDSHIP AND LOVE.

THE heart is peopled by friendship's eye,
    The soul is moved by love;
Under the sky all friendships die;
    Love ever glows above.

Friendship is nothing, love is all;
    The world was dead when love was born:
Love is the soul, which flees our fall;
    Friendship was made for love to scorn.

JAMES T. BRADY.

TOO soon, alas! the link is broken,
    Too soon the days of friendship o'er;
Too soon, oh death! it must be spoken,
    Our own dear BRADY is no more.

The summer heat will come and go,
    The rolling surge will spend its spray,
And gentle winds will softly blow
    Along the beach of Rockaway;

But not for him who paced its shore,
    In love to hear its breaker's sound;
He'll see, alas! that beach no more,
    No more his footprints there be found.

Farewell, my friend of hand and heart,
    Above thy grave let daisies bloom;
The strain which drew our souls apart
    Bowed love and sorrow at thy tomb.

Thou wert the idol of thy race ;
 Genius was jealous of her son,
And, finding none to fill thy place,
 She claimed the laurels thou hadst won.

DO NOT ASK ME.

Do not ask me, pet, I pray,
  Why I linger, why I stay ;
There's no longer left for me
Face or form I care to see.

Save one image in my heart,
Save that figure's counterpart,
Which, as cup of rosy wine,
Makes my life and love divine.

Absence never friendship killed,
Love reflected, never chilled ;
Therefore, sweet, this maxim hold,
And thy love will ne'er grow cold.

Love is nectar, nectar's love,
As my lips to thine will prove—
Prove like roses, tip to tip,
With love's dewdrop on each lip.

DO NOT ASK ME.

If my passion I repress,
Do not think I love thee less;
In its furnace thou shalt find
It has left the dross behind.

When I view thee in the glass
Of my bosom, as thou pass,
Thy religion, I can see,
Holds a tender thought for me.

Love is fancy in undress,
Warm to touch and hot to press;
And that fancy, velvet-toed,
Makes my heart a beaten road.

Love is never free from pain,
And the reason we complain,
What we find to please the eye
Makes us long and pant and sigh.

Do not ask me, pet, I pray,
If my love has died away;
While I dwell upon my fair,
Such a question is despair.

SELF-COMMUNING.

HERE I stand upon Eternity's verge,
  The All-Unknown, whose sombre depth is
    space,
And the wind its walls. For that light I ask
That's more than day. It coldly shuns my quest;
While on me fall the vastness and distress
Of nothingness. Within me rules the spirit
Of unrest, as on flouting time is breathed
The substance of my life—a boon no more
Shall I reclaim, if fitful life's a boon
To him that spurns its narrow paths and curbing
Bounds. The universe is but the purse-string
Of my thoughts, which, from the vast, no conclu-
    sions
Draw, save that I am an atom; of what,
I know not; for what, I know not; nor can
The mind reveal. The gray frost of scoffing
Years has passed behind my destination,

And still all shapes their mysteries hug, and darker
Spread the vail. There's naught defined or reason
Tuned. 'Gainst my judgment's eye a world of
 worlds
Is set. No word had I in my creation.
Since die I must, why should I first exist?
Why this earth's probation of pain, and doubt,
And longing? Why was I first born to earth,
And not to heaven? Yet, if joy is not alloy
Without, wherefore Paradise? Alloy's the salt
Of listless ease, and phlegm, and sloth, as air
Conditions all the solar heat. Without
An opposite, naught can be discerned.
The world is ruled by negatives. Alone
By negatives is harmony produced;
Negative is man, negative is space,
Negative is every aspiration.
The cold must temper heat, and heat the cold.
'Tis opposition in the elements
That tills the earth and feeds its plants and flowers.
Opposite are all nature's primal laws.
Alone from this are love and worship born

Between the sexes. Nor love nor worship
Elsewhere can be proved. Man can not worship
Man; nor woman, woman. We can not feast
On that we do not eat. We can not worship
That we have not seen. The magnet eye alone
Draws worship to the soul. Diverging types
Alone converge to nature's will and law.
Is heaven, then, a place for languor and decay?
The name is false—a bribe to ignorance,
To act an honest part to all mankind,—
A duty born to all, save brutish breasts.

   Within my mental vision I find no ray
Its light to shed upon abysmal thought.
The sun and moon are orbs that give me light;
My friends they are, and yet I know them not.
Relief I find along the spirit air;
It comes from good men's prayers. Still I know it
    not;
While into human or angelic figure
Mold it I would, and, in speech full earnest,
Entreat its inspiration and advice.

   The rugs and wraps of summer winds protect

Me from the solar heat and cool my blood.
Space, the food of winds, has knowledge of me;
Space gives me to the winds to soothe or chill;
The winds know me—not I the winds—because
They nip or fan me, which I can not requite.

   O, dream of dreams, my dream in mystic life!
That floats me midway in soft and stoic
Air, in trance or spell divine, disjoining
Soul from body, all mundane thought from rest
Supernal, till the breath of Jove with incense
Fills my soul! O, solace of mystic dreams,
Which all unrobes me of my leaden cares!
Sweetness, and balm, and joy are thine to give;
Sweetness and perfume from thy budding lips
Dilate my soul, and waft my senses high!
Bright as seraph that sheds a light from heaven
On him whose dreams are stretched beyond the
    spheres!
Fragrant and rare as spiced winds from the South!
Joy of my spirit, mystic life thou art!
Charmed is the balm thy dulcet dreams impart.
From whence come thy delights I crave to know,

Thou touchstone of my soul's divinity?
They come in the morn, ere the voice of man
Shake and dispel the slumber of the air;
They come at eventide, when the silent dew
Descends, as a blessing, on the hot robes
Of retiring day; and they come when all
The flowing drapery of the sky is spread
Before its mirror, that vestal nun, the moon.
In them I find an inspiration found
Not in books of best and wisest men.
A glory to my senses the roses
Of mystic life expand, and the inmost
Chambers of my soul are tenanted with
Seraphim, reposing on beds elysian.
Unbless me of this dream, and I am naught,
Save a speck in fortune's eye, by sullen
Doubts tossed upon reflection's tear and woe.

 Unknown life, filled with fancies and with shrouds,
And dark creations, which are fiends fantastic
To my truer self, and into wizard
Sadness awe me, and self-desertion, till,
In the strength of my weakness, I am lost.

While conscious weakness nurses force and will,
Man is the shadow; and the shadow, man.
By himself, not of himself, he lives, moves,
Thinks, and dreams, and steeps and melts his hours
    away.
His pith is weakness in his maddened rage;
And a fly's wing might his wild passion rule.
  Turning to youth, I gaze upon his face.
His bright eyes glow with innocence and joy;
His silken locks inspire the air with zephyrs
Heavenly. He's all divine from heaven's hand.
His beauty brings me grief, for that beauty
Will not last. Care and trouble too soon will
Come, to rain their misery upon his brow.
Oh, the gloom, the sadness, and the longing!
The dawn—the light—the nothing!
Oh, heart! oh, soul! Where's that joyful kingdom
Of my days, o'er whose flowery lawns and vistas
Fair the winds from heaven my breast with music
    thrilled?—
When to the fulness of its glory rose
My soul, in the joy of its sovereignty;

And on its radiant vision refulgent
Shone the fated star of hope, when love was hope,
And gentle eyes were dreams of bliss, and all
Things breathed a prayer for courteous peace continued?
That was the time to die: in time of joy
To part with joy, and shun its waiting sorrow;
Ere in the tender heart were built dark caves,
For vulpine thought to dwell in and look back.
   Life and death are only one, for life is
Death to think upon.
                      What's this narrow world?
A surging sea of drowning men, who snap,
And snarl, and bite, even while they sink, in lust
Of fame and gold and visions of the heart.
The future is but the past. All is mist
And vapor, and turbulence of the mind.
The world's glory is as a drop of water
On the sand; a city's grandeur passes
Like a flash on the breath of time. Towers
And castles vanish like dewdrops in the sun.
'Tis to the past we build, not the future;

All our plans and toil we leave behind us.
As onward we move, 'tis only to strike
The weary breast 'gainst the frost of sorrow.
The rocks and hills are but the snuff of time;
With time's finger we touch them, and they crumble.
The mind outlives whatever it may see,
For thinking eyes turn all things into dust.
The hope and beauty of the universe
In the stern shadows of reflection die.
We sweat and bear the burdens of a day,
Then close the eyes in sleep forevermore.
Life and death are poised on fate, outreaching
Far the valid clutch of reason's fingers,
As thought grinds thought to nothing. Our flesh dies
On our bones, our nails wither, and our limbs
Are forsaken by the vigor of our days.
Let censuring thought, we crave, be dumb,
While the past, like an arid desert, burns
Our gazing eyeballs. From the scorching present
We onward fly to a future of doubt and haze.

The seasons come; the seasons go; they blossom,

They fade and bloom again. We're born; we blossom,
And we die. Why not bloom again, like that
Nature, of which we are the soul's essence?
Return to life is nature's vital function
But fulfilled. Our spirits walk the deep,
Or skim the air, as living breath is mingled
With the winds. The world's a grave. Again we live
On human clay. We are the dead returned
Again to life.
    A faith we reach and hold,
But not the proof, that something rules beyond
Our gift to know. And yet to know would be
To doubt. We doubt the things we see; we doubt
The words we speak; we doubt the life within,
Ere we move our limbs to prove that we exist.
Even then we doubt. Thought's marrow is a dream.
We live in the shambles of a reason
That's questioned by a closer reason still.
Knowledge is doubt; life is fate; fate is dust.
Greatness is greatest unexplained. Clothe dwarfs
In mystery, and time will make them giants.

Learning pulverizes the living clay,
And to coin a thought fulfils an aspiration.
  The world's a skiff on the river Time,
And all are pilots, with diverging aims.
Our brightest dream, gently rocked on the wave
Of thought, palmy and blithe, is but the fleeting
Spell of wan and wild-eyed sorrow's hectic
Glow, which bears the soul, with muffled oar, be-
    yond
A fated sea, to rest from human woe.
  Hill and dale, mountain and savanna,
In busy life I view. Where'er the eye
May roam, the countless herds graze and prosper;
The fruitful fields are laden with their gifts,
And Mother Earth is dressed in vernal robes;
While her daughter, Spring, with buds of hope
That mother's breast adorns. And all for what?
For me to contemplate the passing scene,
And in that contemplation have the balm
Of pleasure's peace chilled by winds from open
    graves;
To contemplate man's tongue as the mind's bell,

And his mouth the stomach's hopper; to gild
With fancy a fond imagination :
Making all space a universe of life ;
Marshalling its plains with warriors of eld ;
Awe-struck at Jehovah, in a chariot
Of stars, crowned by His suns, attempered by
His moons, and comets for His waving plumes.
  Tyrant custom forever censures light.
Craven worship, with its snares, is but the craft
Of kings, who draw it down from mystery
To themselves, more loyal their slaves to hold.
Fear no worship is, but cowardice rank,
The slave's habiliment ; while learning is
Prejudice ; and ignorance, superstition.
As brazen suns aggrieve the heavenly stars,
The soul divine is scourged by bigots' tongues.
All is light of nothing.
                  The trust of youth
Is lost in the haze of age. To be unhappy
Is to read and learn. When all is known that
Can be known, we fail to hold a vision.
Fog, waste, dissolution are all that time

Can bring. We trust to-morrow, and distrust
To-day. And life is this, and death: to-day
Is death; to-morrow, life—the life of clay.
Away we float on the dark wing of time,
And naught remains, save the mockery of dust.

   Nature, God, and Man are the trinity
Divine. One is all, and all are one. 'Tis
The God within us, not without, our deepest
Reverence claims, which is to know and ourselves
Esteem as the only gods; nor suffer
This earth a king or slave endure. Wherefore
Shall man worship? Worship the sin
That brought him on this earth! What juggling
    fraud
On Reason's God! Wherefore have we reason,
Save to understand? Howe'er we may our
Sense befog in mist of superstition
And creeds insensate, the strong and steady eye
Of discerning reason the mist dispels,
And challenges the proof, lifting the mind
Above the weight of matter. My godhead
Reason is. Shall I forswear my godhead,

And live a lie?—live a dumb creation,
And place in contradictions tortuous all
My spiritual trust, to sink beneath my
Mental current of disdain? How can man,
Enlightened, his clear judgment's depths cajole,
And live a hypocrite? He's reason blind
Who reasons not, and tyrant he who demands
Our worship. There is a fabled power
All mercy claims. Before his godly eyes
Are moaning babes in flames of fire consumed;
Yet speaks he not, nor moves he in that love
That sinful mortal might. Of jealous traits
He is, and only him shall worship all, while
Half the world by gross idolatry all
Senses shame; and yet the fabled wisdom
Guides them not, but would them punish
For that they know not of—a creature damn
For light he never saw!
      To the minds that
Rise above their fellows, naught is real, save
Imagination. Of life 'tis the essence.
It gives to the palate, taste; to the heart, pulse;

To the soul, trust ; and to the will, conquest.
It gives to genius bold that assertion
That succeeds and all the world surprises.
   The orb of day ascends, and glows, and fades,
As man, his youth, meridian, and decline.
Fear is our habitation, and frail hope
The door, through which we pass to joy still-born,
On dark tides of rising sorrow.   Never
At rest, never at peace, till the last gleam
Of flickering light flies the socket.   And where
The end?   Perhaps in this: When time makes
    havoc
With our last remains, their first consignment
Being to worms and putrefaction, their next
To dust, we're blown by whistling winds into
The eye of him that preaches.

A HIDDEN SORROW.

SAD in the morning, sad in the night,
　　My life is passed away;
For me this world has no delight,
　　Nor hope a single ray.

Pale in the shade of fancied wrong
　　I yield before thy frown,
While round my life misfortunes throng,
　　And clouds my sorrows crown.

To thee my soul was ever true,
　　I lived for thee alone;
If other gentle eyes I knew,
　　They made thee more mine own.

Let not thy pride deny my prayer;
　　On bended knee and low,
I lay my soul's afflictions bare,
　　For none but thee to know.

A HIDDEN SORROW.

Let not thy breast with woes consume,
    Nor brood o'er grievance dead;
My wayward love was fiction's bloom,
    Whose leaves were teardrops shed.

If anger should thy bosom burn,
    Or sorrow cloud thy mind,
To by-gone days O fondly turn,
    And there thy solace find.

Turn to the days when all the land
    Was balmed with rosy air,
When two fond hearts strolled hand in hand,
    Unknown to strife or care.

Thy soul I drank from out those eyes
    That still diviner grew,
Till love, united, reached the skies,
    And God pronounced it true.

We loved broad nature, fresh and fair,
    We loved our silence, too,
For love that's true, professions spare—
    Love's golden words are few.

When grief now falls upon thy breast,
  Or sorrow dims thine eye,
Upon thy bosom let me rest,
  Or with that sorrow die.

ADIEU.

THOUGH cold the word, it must be spoken,
   Though crushed the heart and deep the sigh;
Though every chord of friendship's broken,
   At last it comes—the low good-by.

Sadder than death that word to me,
   Sadder than dreams beyond the grave;
Yet in its sound I know I'm free,
   Ah, free to be my freedom's slave.

Our happy days our sorrows count,
   Pleasure's the measure of our pain,
And dreams of youth the flowing fount
   That pours those sorrows back amain.

When winds were light and days were bright,
   There came no breath our joys to mar;
I knew no morn, I knew no night,
   You were to me a noonday star.

But time, ah, time, what changes bring!
　　What mysteries strange we leave behind!
Like ivy old, sad memories cling
　　Around the ruins of the mind.

Memory, through its mist of years,
　　Like struggling moonbeams through the cloud,
Or fitful smiles through pressing tears,
　　In mockery gleams above my shroud.

While still to me the world seems fair,
　　And nature fresh in all its bloom,
I nurse the viper of despair,
　　I live but in the future's gloom.

My hopes in life forever gone,
　　The joys of youth long past recall,
A mournful waste, I still live on,
　　Nor caring now how soon I fall.

Farewell, dear friend—it must be said;
　　The time has come for you and me
To lay our friendships with the dead,
　　And life resign to fate's decree.

www.ingramcontent.com/pod-product-compliance
Lightning Source LLC
Chambersburg PA
CBHW031346160426
43196CB00007B/745